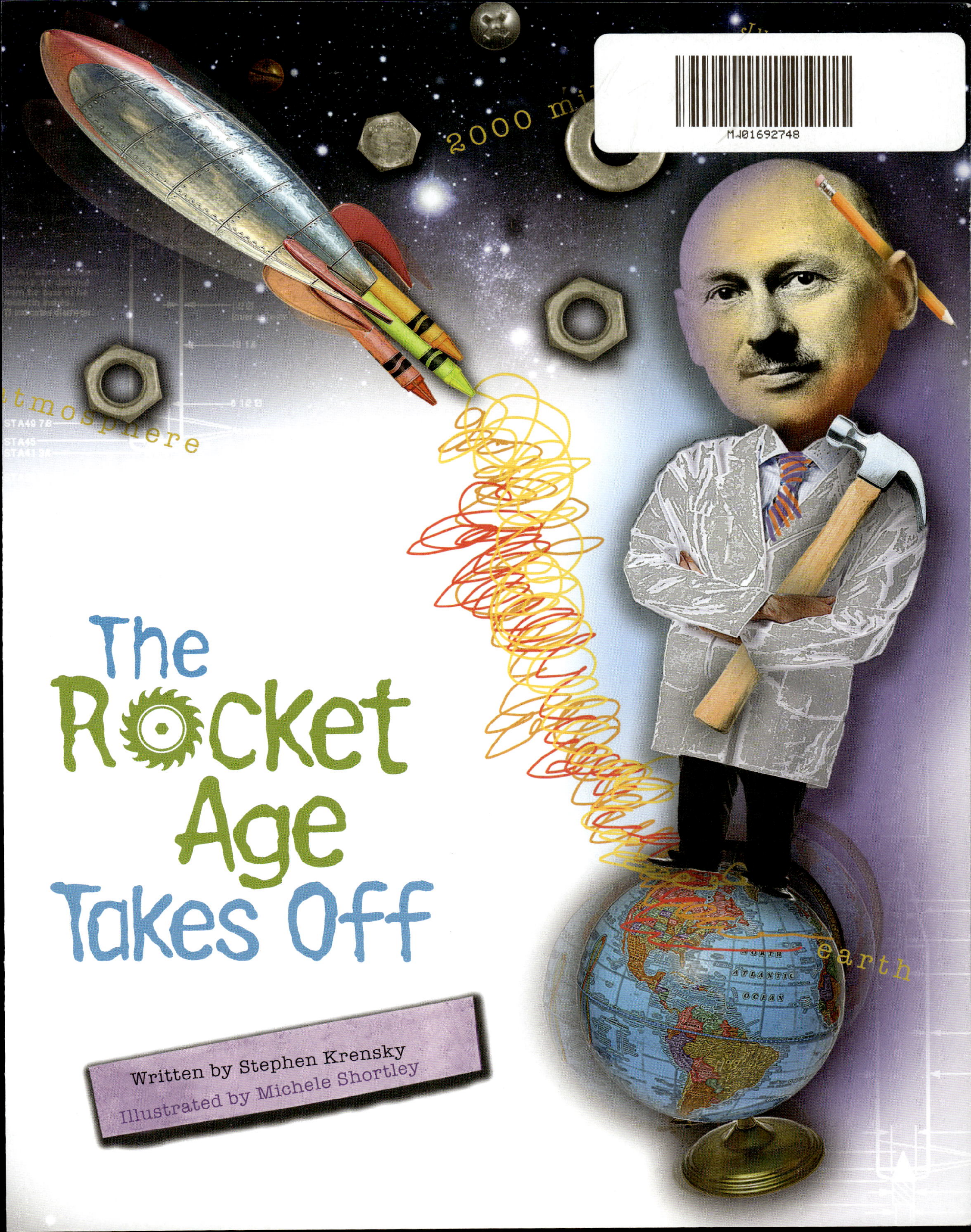

The Rocket Age Takes Off

Written by Stephen Krensky
Illustrated by Michele Shortley

This book was developed by SAE International in partnership with Education Development Center, Inc., through funding from Nissan North America, Inc., for the *A World In Motion®* program. For more information on the *A World In Motion* program, please visit www.awim.org.

We would like to acknowledge KidsKnowIt Network for the astronomy jokes included in this book.

All NASA photos are courtesy of nasaimages.org. NASA images are located on cover (Dr. Goddard's face), page 1 (antique car and rocket), page 3 (Nell), page 9 (Dr. Goddard and Nell), page 19 (Dr. Goddard), page 20 (moon), page 22 (Nell), page 23 (Dr. Goddard's face), page 25 (Dr. Goddard's face), page 26 (moon), back cover (Dr. Goddard's face).

For permission and licensing requests, contact:

SAE Permissions
Address: 400 Commonwealth Drive
Warrendale, PA 15096-0001 USA
E-mail: copyright@sae.org
Phone: 724-772-4028
Fax: 724-772-9765

To purchase bulk quantities, contact:

SAE Customer Service
E-mail: CustomerService@sae.org
Phone: 877-606-7323 *(USA and Canada)*
724-776-4970 *(outside USA)*
Fax: 724-776-1615

International Standard Book Number (ISBN) 978-0-7680-3489-9
Library of Congress Control Number (LCCN) 2010937031

SAE International®
400 Commonwealth Drive
Warrendale, PA 15096-0001 USA

It was a good thing

Robert Goddard didn't mind the cold. The winter of 1926 was harsh at his Aunt Effie's farm, and he had already been out there several times. The farm was only a couple of miles from his home in Worcester, Massachusetts, but they were long miles in bitter weather.

On some of the trips, Dr. Goddard had gone in a horse-drawn wagon. On others, he had traveled by car. But always he carried the same thing carefully packed away in the back.

A liquid-propelled rocket.

Dr. Goddard had named

his rocket Nell. It had taken years to design her and build all the necessary equipment. But that did not bring success by itself. Launching Nell properly had turned out to be difficult.

One time Nell had fallen over to the left.

Another time she had fallen over to the right.

And just a week earlier, a fizzled launch had jammed Nell into the frame that supported her, damaging them both.

nebula
Nell
fizzled
launch
puff
3

$E=mc^2$
E is energy
m is mass
c is the speed of light
in a vacuum
SPACE

Q: What do you get when you cross a comet with a guppy?
A: A starfish.

But Dr. Goddard did not

get discouraged easily. Born in 1882, he had often been sick growing up. Some of these illnesses lasted for months, and he had developed great patience to get through them. Even so, by the time he reached high school, young Bob was two years behind the other students his age.

Science was always his passion, though. Bob was constantly tinkering with one thing or another. He had tried to turn graphite into diamonds and experimented with light-weight aluminum balloons. He even devoted considerable time building a perpetual motion machine, which, had he ever succeeded, would have run forever.

Q: How many balls of string would it take to reach the moon?
A: One very large ball.

At sixteen, Bob read

H.G. Wells' science fiction novel *The War of the Worlds.* It told the story of how Martians invaded the Earth in their spaceships and very nearly destroyed humankind. As Wells described the events, they seemed very believable. The book made Bob think more about outer space and what it would be like to go there.

The next year Bob climbed a cherry tree to cut off some dead branches. At one point he looked down at the ground and suddenly had a thought. He imagined "how wonderful it would be to make some device which had even the possibility of ascending to Mars, and how it would look on a small scale, if sent up from the meadow at my feet."

The atmosphere of the Sun (called the chromosphere) is hotter than its surface.

And now, twenty-seven

years later, Dr. Goddard was still working in that direction. But even he had to admit that Nell looked a bit crude. She was ten feet long and held in place by a triangular skeleton. On top were the motor and the combustion chamber, which would be shot into the sky. Below that on each side were the two propellant tanks. Narrow pipes connected them to the chamber above.

Nell weighed a little over five pounds on her own and five more when loaded with fuel. The motor was at the top because Dr. Goddard thought that placing it there would provide greater stability in flight. (When Dr. Goddard realized this design didn't help, he moved the motor in later models to its more modern position under the rocket.)

Q: What did the cat do when he got dirty in Dr. Goddard's workshop?

A: He took a meteor shower.

gasoline line
liquid oxygen line
rocket motor
liquid oxygen tank
gasoline tank
rocket bits
5 pounds!

Fireworks originated in China.
The entire Great Wall, stretches about 5,500 miles.
The Giant Panda, a native to China, eats 99% bamboo.

Rockets had been

originally developed in China. As early as 1232, the Chinese used them while fighting their frequent enemies, the Mongols. (The name rocket itself came from the Italian word rochetta, a small firecracker first manufactured in 1379.)

The Chinese rockets were made of bamboo tubes. They were sealed at one end and filled with gunpowder. The tubes were tied to long sticks planted in the ground. When a fuse ignited the gunpowder, the mixture of fire and gas shot out the open end. The force of the blast propelled the tubes high into the air. They rained down on the Mongols, injuring some and probably scaring the rest.

The Mongols were "bamboo"zled.

Q: What kind of star wears sunglasses?
A: Movie star.

The 15-star flag flew over Fort McHenry during the War of 1812.

As rocket science

improved, the rockets themselves became more powerful. By the early 1800s, the British scientist Sir William Congreve had invented an iron rocket that could fly 9,000 feet. During the War of 1812, a war between Great Britain and the United States, the British navy famously used Congreve's rockets, firing them on Ft. McHenry outside Baltimore, Maryland.

One witness to this attack was the young lawyer Francis Scott Key. He composed a poem about the battle. Among the things he could see "by the dawn's early light" were the "rockets' red glare." His words later became the lyrics to the "Star Spangled Banner."

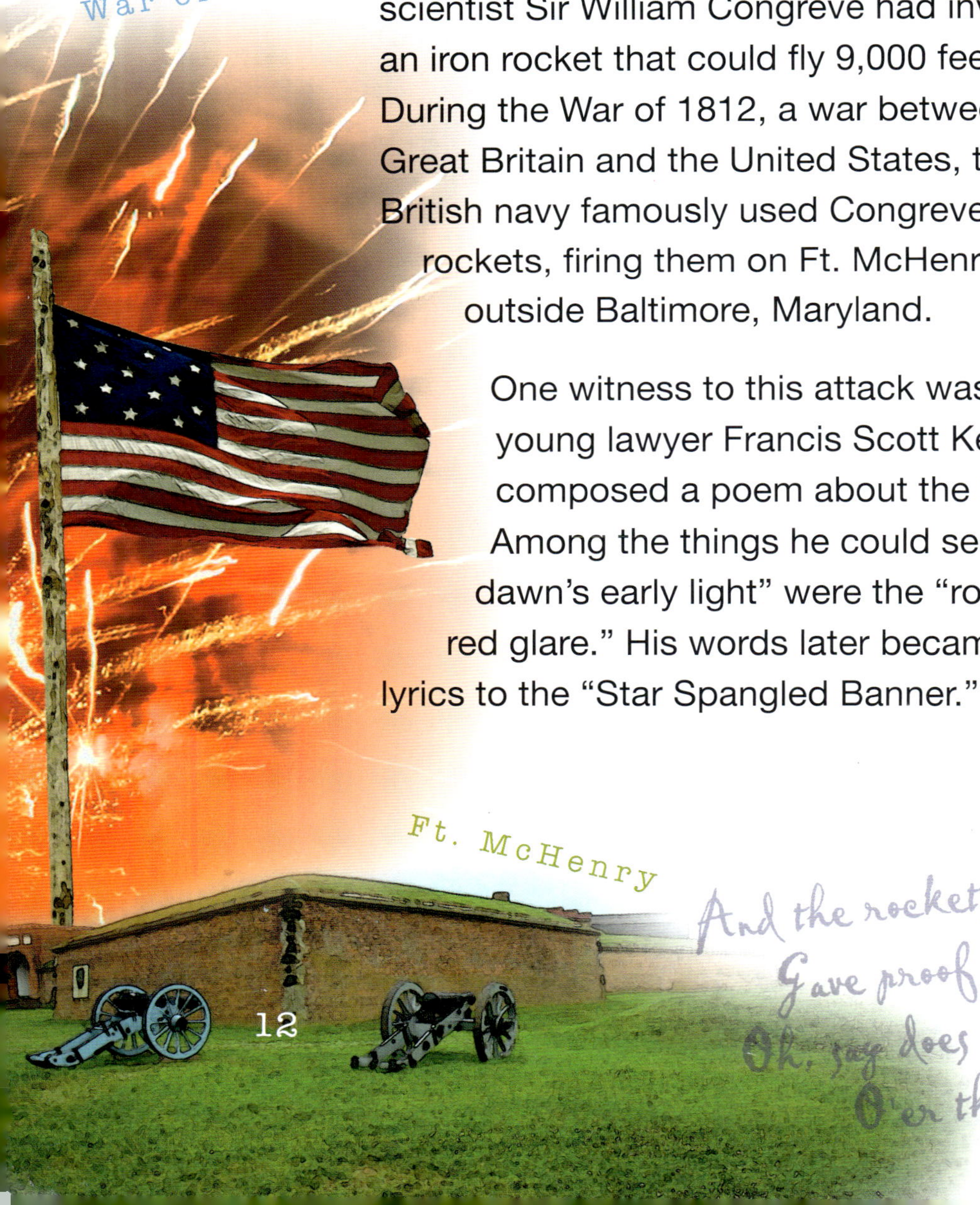

Ft. McHenry

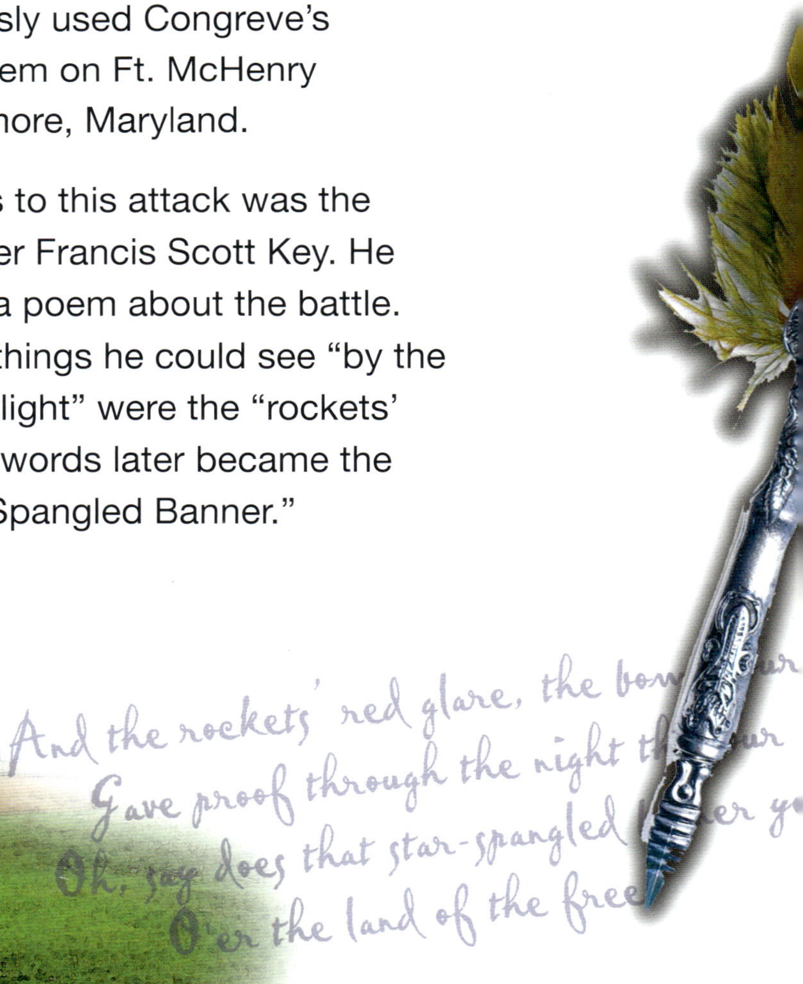

g in air,
g was still there.
wave

The Civil War started in 1861. That same year The Great Comet (one of eight in the 19th century) was visible.

Q: What do you call a multi-colored cannon?
A: ART-illary

It was not surprising

that rockets were used in wars because they had much in common with another weapon—the cannon. Both devices created an explosion inside a metal tube that was open at one end.

But there was one very important difference between the two. In a cannon, the explosion inside the tube propelled a cannon ball into the air. In a rocket, the explosion sent the tube itself—the rocket—flying.

The size of the explosion also mattered a lot. The bigger it was, the farther a rocket or cannonball would fly. Of course, the explosion had to be controlled and predictable. Otherwise, the rocket or cannon could be easily damaged or destroyed.

So the challenge

facing all early rocket designers was how to give the rockets enough thrust, enough power to soar safely high into the air. In the 1890s, a Russian scientist named Konstantin Tsiolkovsky determined that exploding gunpowder would never provide enough energy to lift a large rocket. And any kind of fuel in a gas form would be too bulky to store on the rocket itself as it lifted off. (Tsiolkovsky kept his ideas to himself, though, so other scientists did not learn of them till many years later.)

Liquid fuels, though, held more potential. Manageable amounts, ignited in the right way, could generate significant power. Dr. Goddard independently came to the same conclusion in the years leading up to his attempted launches. He also determined that the most promising liquid fuels were a mixture of hydrogen and oxygen.

liquid fuel
It is really hopping with these liquid fuels!
gunpowder (not enough energy)
gas (storage too heavy)

faster than
a sugar rush

But knowing liquid fuels

were needed did not solve all the challenges Dr. Goddard faced. Three of his specific advances came from his research between 1908 and 1923.

1 First, he pioneered using a steam nozzle in conjunction with the combustion chamber to direct the flow of hot gases in the right direction.

2 Second, he explored at what speed the fuel should be sent into the combustion chamber. Establishing the proper flow or pressure was important to creating the most effective explosion.

3 And third, he proposed the use of multiple stages to send his rocket aloft. As the fuel in each stage was used up, the stage itself would fall away from the rocket. That way the active rocket would not have to carry the dead weight from the parts that were already used up.

Using such designs,

Goddard boldly concluded that a rocket could someday fly to the moon. Many critics, including the editorial writers at the newspaper the *New York Times*, laughed at this idea. They didn't believe that any rocket could work in the vacuum of space because they assumed that in a vacuum there would be nothing for the force of the burning fuel to push against. And they made fun of Dr. Goddard for lacking the basic "knowledge ladled out daily in high schools."

Milky Way
What are the cows' favorite things in our solar system? The moooooooons.
Newton's 3rd law: For every action there is an equal and opposite reaction.
reaction: balloon goes up
action: air rushes down

We better head
north early!
ACME
Hot Stuff
Blow Torch
GODDARD
Yo, if that
takes flight,
I'm outta
sight.

Q: What type of music do astronauts like to listen to in space?
A: NepTUNEs.

But Dr. Goddard

remained convinced he was right, and that conviction had brought him to this latest attempt on March 16th. As he and his wife Esther watched, his associate Henry Sachs used a blowtorch to set off the igniter on the top of the motor. Then Sachs lit an alcohol lamp under the fuel tanks. The resulting heat sent the fuel up the pipes into the combustion chamber, and a flame soon appeared at the end of the nozzle.

So many years of work came down to this one moment.

Q: When do astronauts have lunch?
A: At launch time.

Dr. Goddard himself

wrote down what happened next. "The rocket did not rise at first, but the flame came out, and there was a steady roar. After a number of seconds, it rose slowly until it cleared the frame, and then at express-train speed, curving over to the left, and striking the ice and snow, still going at a rapid rate. It looked almost magical as it rose, without any appreciably greater noise or flame, as if it said, 'I've been here long enough; I think I'll be going someplace else if you don't mind.'"

Score one for Goddard!

In the end, Nell rose forty-one feet into the air in two and a half seconds before her fuel was exhausted and she fell back to earth.

Go baby go!

The Apollo 11 mission landed the first humans on the moon.

Before humans, monkeys were launched into space.

Nell's flight that day,

short as it was, truly began the Rocket Age. And further progress came swiftly. Only forty-three years later, a rocket still following Dr. Goddard's basic design carried Apollo 11 to the moon.

Robert Goddard did not live to see that day, but in one way he predicted it. As he noted in a speech he gave at his high school graduation in 1904: "It has often proved true that the dream of yesterday is the hope of today, and the reality of tomorrow."